THIS ADULT
COLORING BOOK
BELONGS TO:

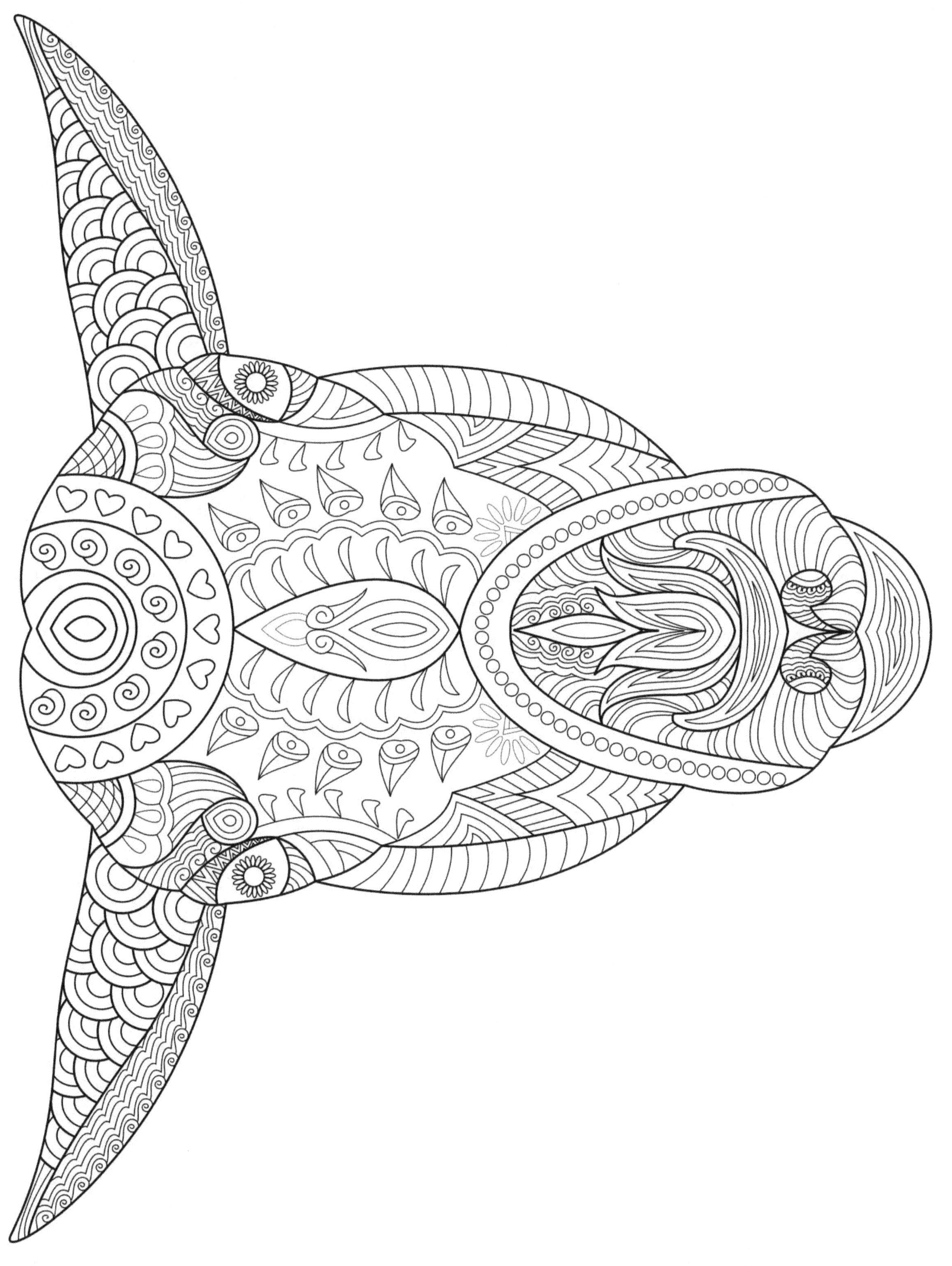

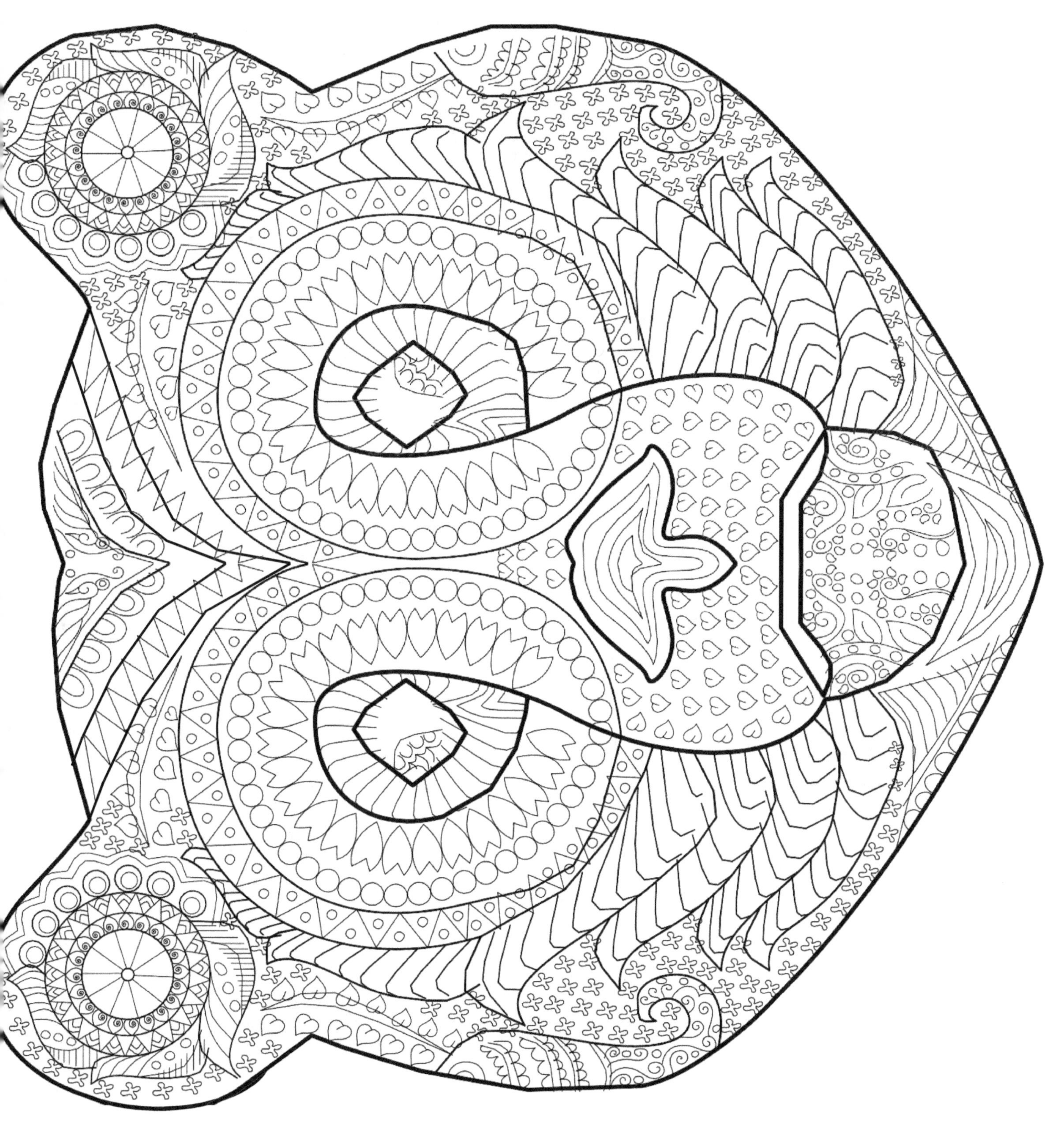

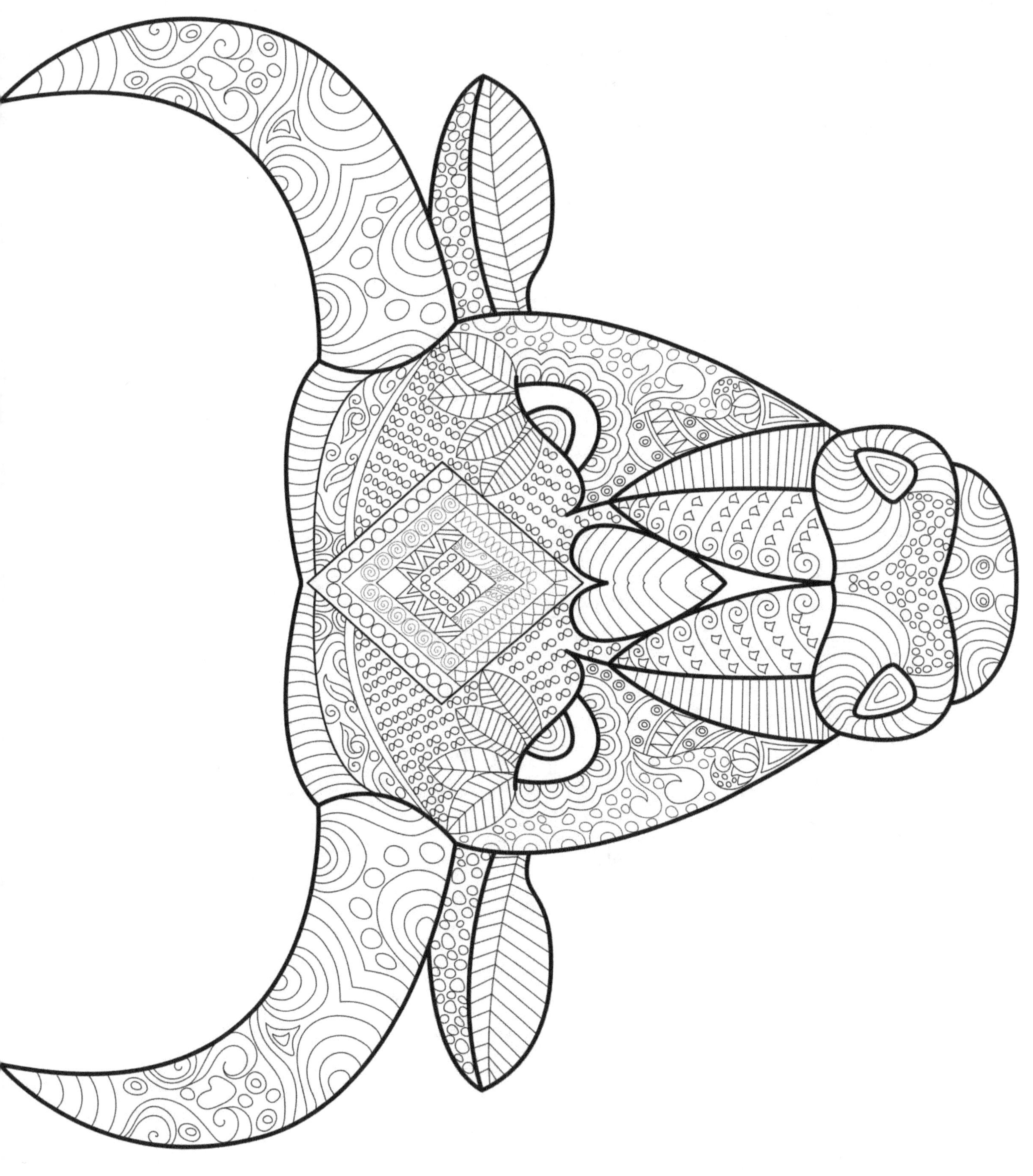

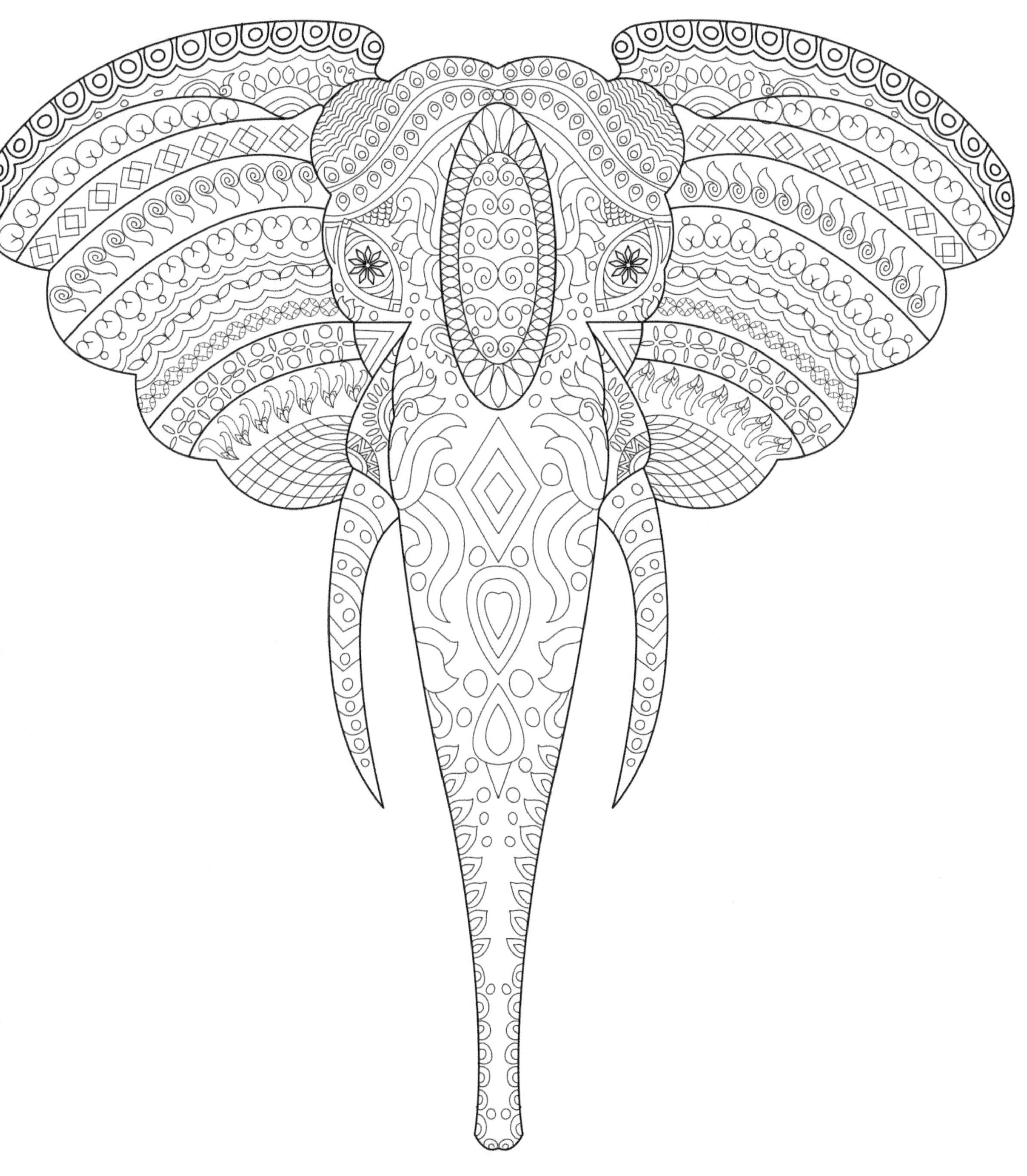

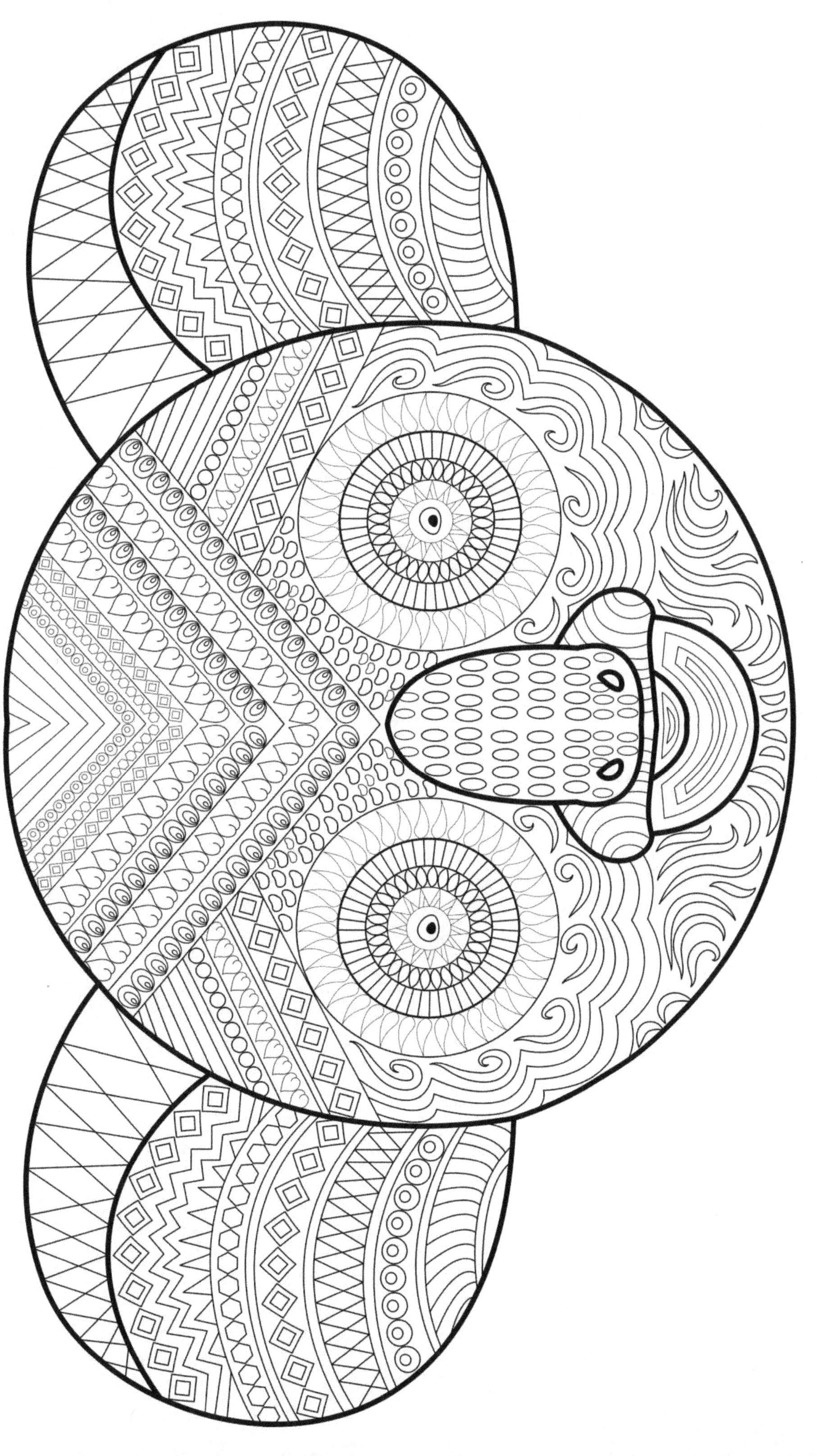

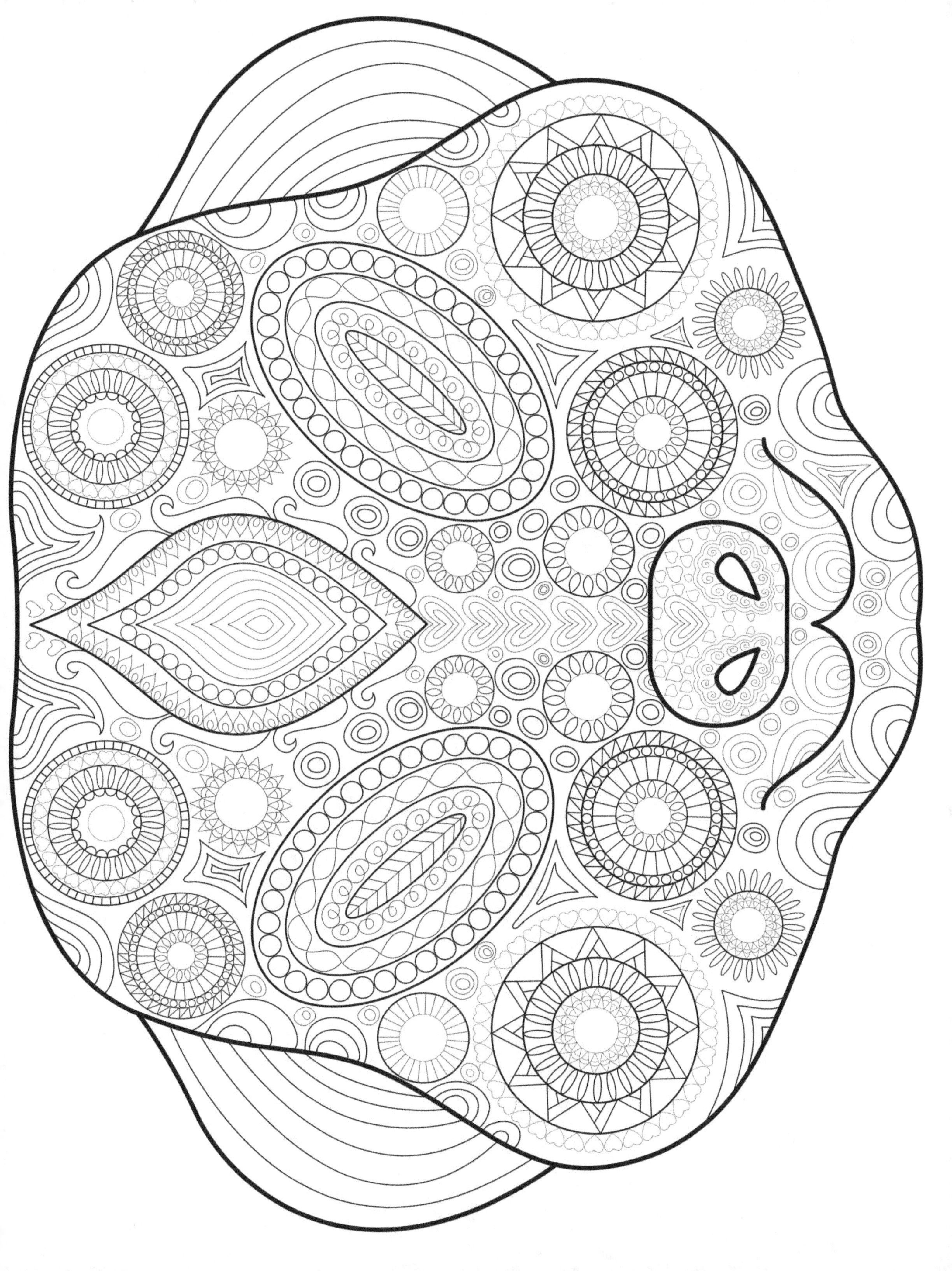

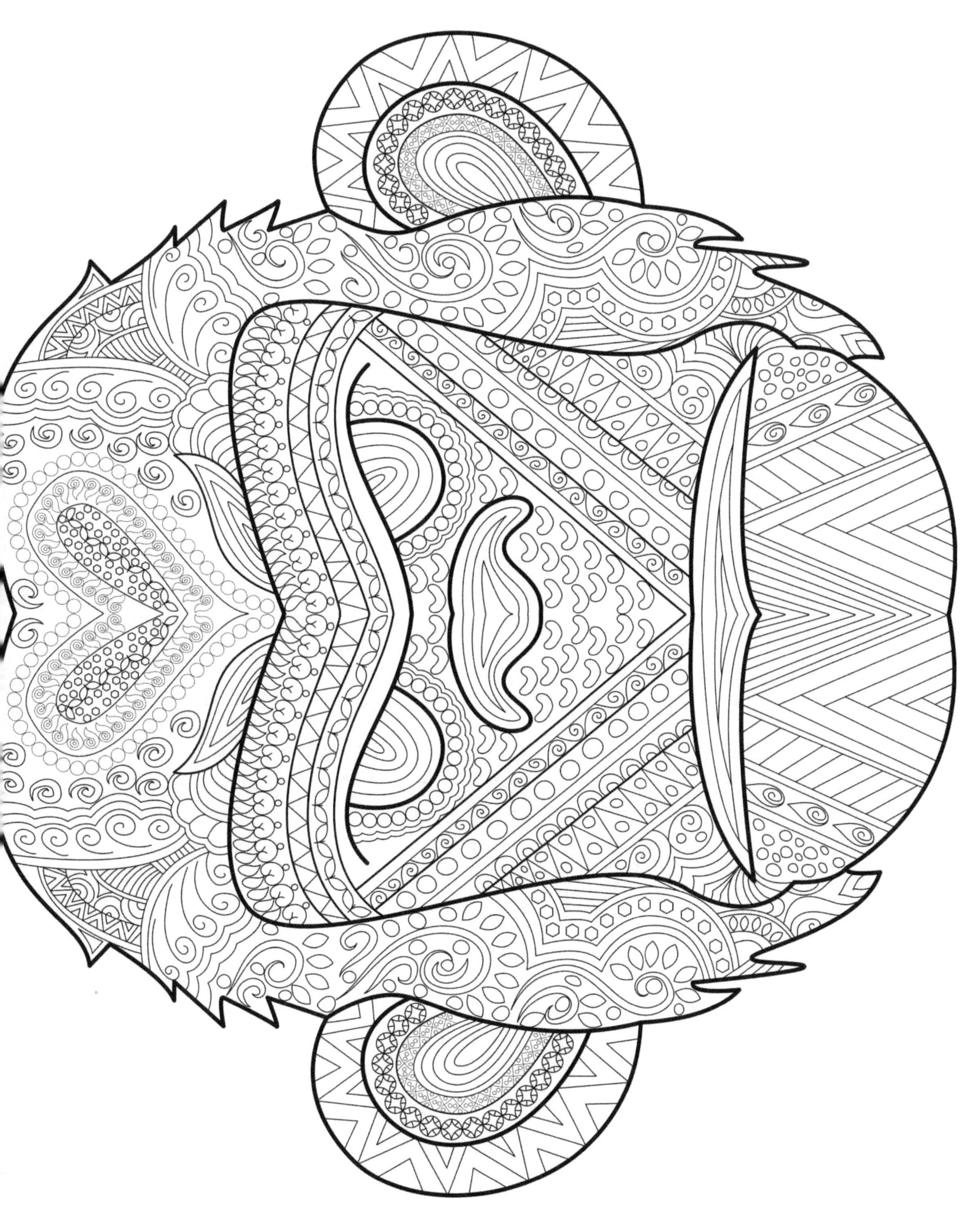

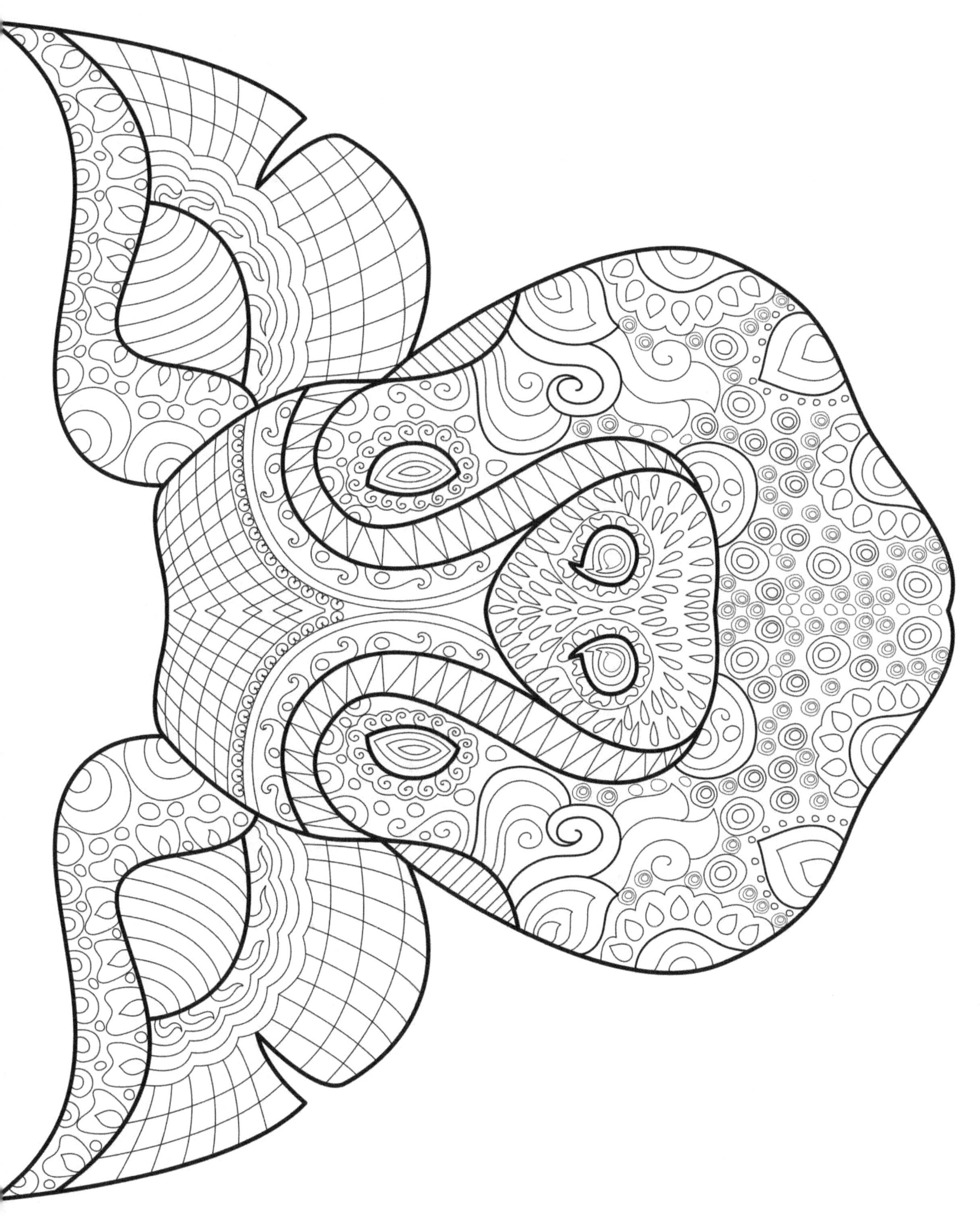

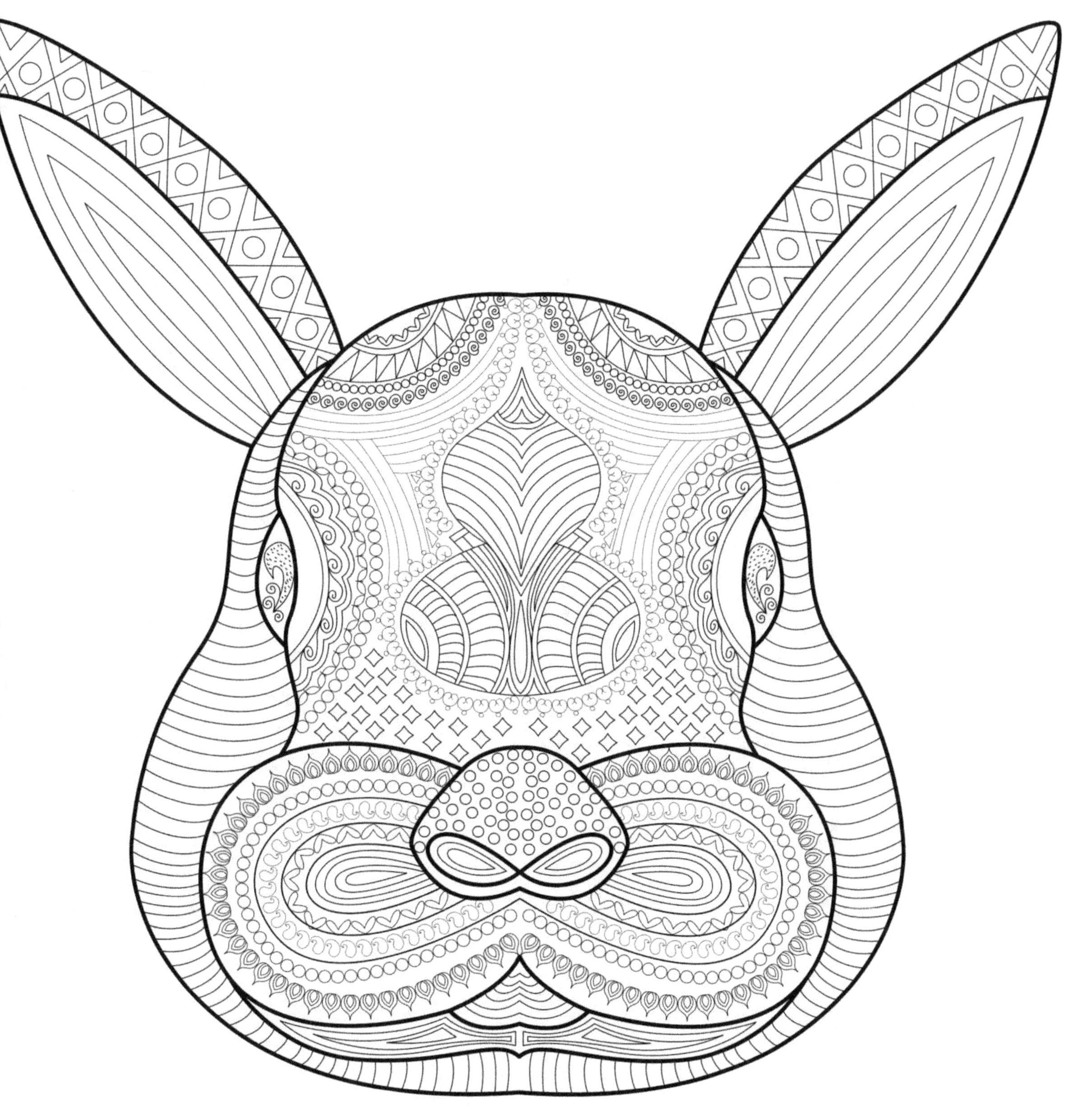

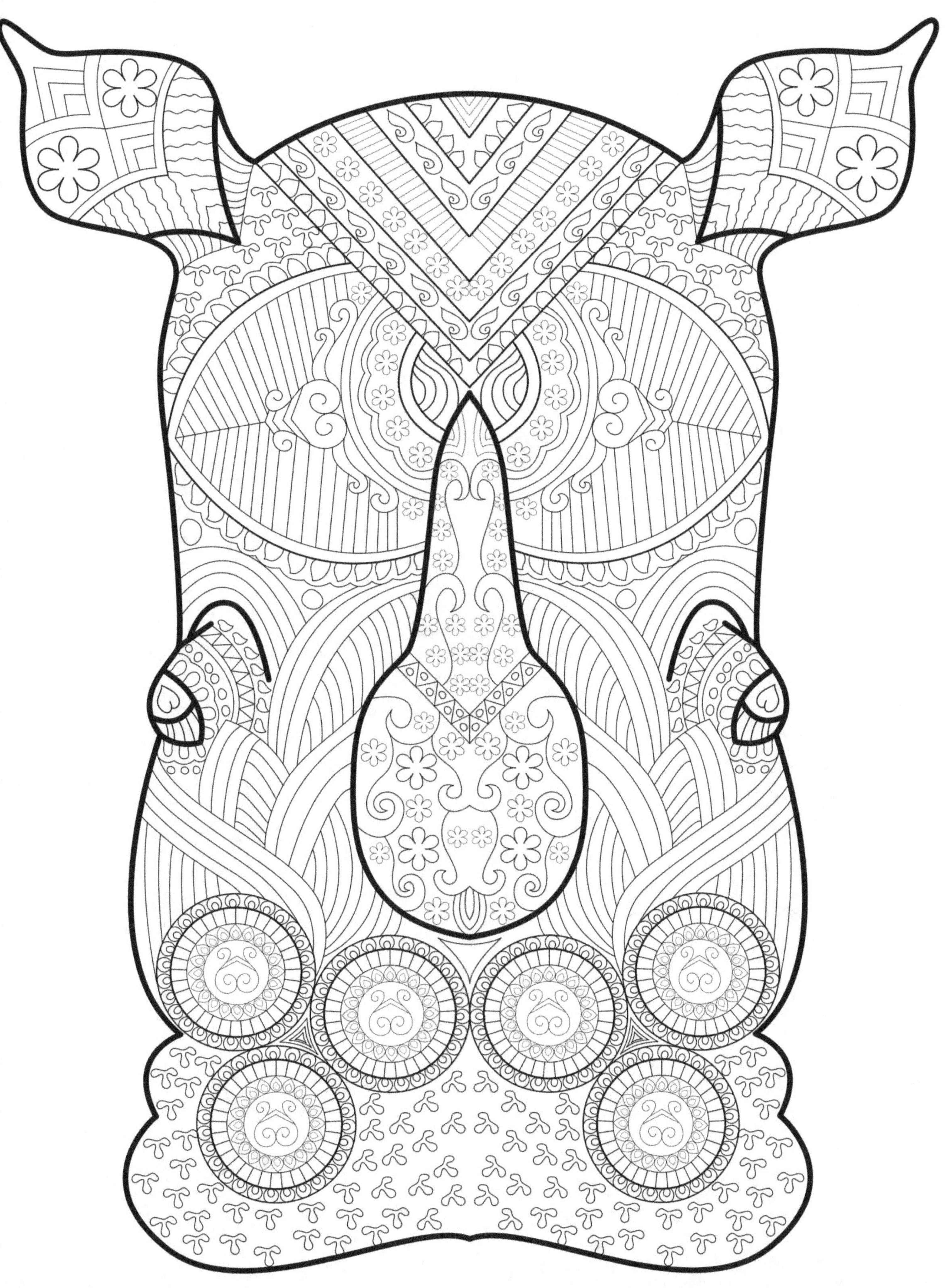

If you enjoyed this book, check out the coloring Books available By

Sassy Scribblez

on Amazon.